Other works by Maria James-Thiaw
(previously published as Maria C. James):

Windows to the Soul
Rising Waters
FREEverse (CD)

Other works published by postDada Press:

The Three Faces of Brahman by Christine O'leary-Rockey
Lolling Along That Meadow . . . a Snow of White Dots by Marty Esworthy
Raw: Exposing the Untamed Mind by John Destalo

Talking "White"

Maria James-Thiaw

iUniverse, Inc.
Bloomington

Talking "White"

iUniverse books may be ordered through booksellers or by contacting:

iUniverse
1663 Liberty Drive
Bloomington, IN 47403
www.iuniverse.com
1-800-Authors (1-800-288-4677)

ISBN: 978-1-4759-7977-0 (sc)
ISBN: 978-1-4759-7978-7 (ebk)

Published in conjunction with postDada Press, Harrisburg, PA

Printed in the United States of America

iUniverse rev. date: 03/06/2013

"Maria James-Thiaw is the beauty and passion of the African Diaspora Writer. She is a storyteller surrounded by a universe of hungry starving listeners, trying to devour her word by word. She is more than you see and all that she can imagine. Maria dares to write poetic stories that most dare not think aloud, because they are not sure how to say it. I love the voice of this Poetic Writer. I know you will too!"

-Nathaniel Gadsden, founder,
Nathaniel Gadsden's Writers Wordshop

Acknowledgements

Special thanks to postDada Press, a division of postDada Media, for believing in my work and helping me share it with the world. Thank you to the many "friends and also-poets" that educate, inspire and provide venues for poetry to flourish. Without you in Central PA I wouldn't have found my voice. In addition, I'd like to thank my phenomenal professors and advisors: Elena Georgiou, Maureen Seaton and Paul Selig from Goddard College, Liz Corcoran and Liz Abrams-Morley from Rosemont College and Marilyn Kallet from the University of Tennessee-Knoxville who invited me to "taste and see" how beautiful a poet's life could be!

The following poems in this collection have been previously published:

- "Aunt Rosie's Gift"—*The Pitkin Review*, Goddard College, Winter 2009
- "Virginia Slims"—*The Sylvan*, Pennsylvania Poetry Society, Fall 2010
- "Big Mamma Blue," "The Blind," "Nigrescent," & "Café On Market"—*Black Magnolias Literary Journal*, Summer 2011
- "Rant of the Backslider," "Double Whammy," and "Addict"—*Love Your Rebellion*, Fall 2011
- "Keeping It Real'" Poetry Ink 2013, April 2013

Contents

The Post-Black Manifesto

"The fact that you don't like how someone else is doing blackness doesn't
mean they aren't black. Blackness is not a club you can be expelled from."
~Touré, Who's Afraid of Post Blackness?

Post-Black is the new black.
Obsidian and centered,
it's spit from full lips,
slips from pen tips;
It will live in your mouth tomorrow.

Forget Webster! Red-backed and
gorged with lies.
Post-Black spreads too wide.
Touré didn't start this. Not Ellis. Not Womack.
It lives in your hood, but it's global;
As American as apple pie and slave shacks.

Post-Black art moves freely
without being house slaved by field slaves,
without being strung up
by the Willie-Lynched.
An international word.
Just a word, and the word, a movement.
It's simplerful*, so don't dread it.
Don't get locked in.

---

*   simplerful—SIMPLe & powERFULL. Something that is both amazingly
     simple and incredibly powerfull. (The Urban Dictionary)

Post-Black psychology
reacts to hood rats with paroxysm,
post-Black lit, post-Black bourgeoisie, and y'all:
The poetry-heads, the afro-futurists,
black leaders arguing about "butt dancin' for Clinton."

Post-Black in response to a war without end;
Post-Black revolution, you friends and also-poets,
ballers, drum makers and mega-church minions.
Post-Black hates hot combs and
plays out in the sun too long.

Post-Black is Harlem, Atlanta and Charlotte.
Post-Black poets talk "white," so they've been told.
They write nature, love, beaches and
can even win gold with pigeon peas in the kitchen.

Post-Blacks have been called bourgeois,
oreo, high yella, and "new"
inspiring eye rolls and "dismuthafuckas" from
haters and wish-I-coulds.

Say post-Black like dada.
Become famous. Achieve eternal bliss.
With head nod and dap,
with a quick terrorist fist bump,
say it till you lose it. Say it till you black out.
Get rid of everything that smacks of
essentialism. Say "Post-Black," because

Post-Black is the world soul.
Post-Black is the point.
Post-Black is the world's best African Black Soap.
Post-Black President Obama.
Post-Black Dr. Cosby
Post-Black Ms. Winfrey.

Boundless, limitless, self-defined,
climbing like New Negroes
on mountains of art,
souls have grown deep,
rooted in, but unrestricted by
blackness.

Reflections

My eyes bounced back and saw myself
reflected in pools of Black ink.
Words climbed up my cheeks
then soaked in.

Street critics, silent and loud,
glared, made me see me—
spawn of my dead grandmother's voice,
with her stay-out-of-the-sun mentality,
Nella Larsoning, imitating life.

Black ink bites.
Leaves scars
        in my face, so
I slammed the poet's book closed
and refuse to look at me anymore.

Ebony in Ivory

Like ivy on ivory I climb,
Reaching for what they've achieved—

prolific prize winners with their
Pushcarts, Pulitzers, presidential precedents—

Reading their bios makes me think I can fly.
Maybe that is the point of it all.

How to Write a Poem

First, find a quiet place, comfortable
and be sure to have your instruments ready:
The pen, your scalpel,
the paper, gleaming white and sanitary.

Decide if you need music to wheel in your thoughts;
What kind? Smooth jazz? Neo-soul? Classical?
Which will best extract the emotion?

And when the idea lies before you,
vibrating with anticipation,
use your pen to dissect it like a surgeon.

Open it up.
Blow air inside, so you can see all its parts.
Pick up pieces,

suture them with similes,
stitch them to metaphor, then cut again
and again and again and again,

until its true meaning spills over, rolls out,
drips onto the floor;
Emotionally saturate the sanitary

till its full context is red and throbbing
in the palm of your hand.

Ravens and Writing Desks

In photos, spheres of light dance
on piano keys.
Poets crane necks to see a desk
hanging like a chandelier.
This must be Wonderland.

Set tables are upside down,
chairs float above our heads,
the menus speak French;
the food has eyes.

The note on a clay jug says,
"Drink me," so I do.
We shrink as time becomes velum
folded over us.
Out from black alleys
and behind old roman pillars
it speaks to us.

Ancient voices hum.
Servant boys stare from boarded windows,
A fat woman folds blankets and hangs them
from a balcony that crumbled centuries ago.
Old bricks cry real tears.

They've seen blood spilled
on these cobblestones.
They've seen horses back up,
whinny and screech,
unwilling to be dragged into war.

But in the studio where we write,
the grape vines are playful, mischievous;
the Virgin statue, nosey.
Someone lives without breathing
outside the bathroom,
and if you stay in the bedroom,
Coltrane plays hits from *Bye Bye Blackbird*
at your bedside.

La Fluer

It's not that he was attractive
with his time-worn face and
très Européen mop of curly hair.
There was no cowboy in him,
no Armani laden capitalist or
Clooney-esque quality.
He wasn't pretty, nor could pecs
be seen under his too respectable
brown-tweed jacket,
and yet in that moment,
he had lassoed the imagination of
every woman in the outdoor café.
It was the way he leaned back in his
plastic chair without questioning
its strength to hold him,
closed his eyes, planted his face
in a thriving blossom
drew in air from his core, and took it all in.
One deep breath inward,
swirling his head so the petals could caress his skin.
He wanted to wear this scent.
as if it were the first scent he'd ever smelled,
or the last he ever would;
As if the scent itself stopped time.
He wrapped it around his head like a turban,
let it dance in his nostrils;
Lapping it up, he was a kitten in milk.
We could see his mind was caressing it
like something fleshy and soft.

He let it envelop him
until the plant itself moaned and quaked in ecstasy.
And I, with a cold blocking my nose,
was merely an envious voyeur,
but my friend, a Rose herself, tired of the feeling
of being stopped up by life's tragedies and demands
marched over to that plant without hesitation,
her words swirling in the dust her feet had left behind,

I'll have what he's having! She demanded. J'aurai ce qu'il a !

Griot's Song

In honor of Leopold Sedar Senghor, poet, co-founder
of La Negritude, and first president of Senegal

Your negritude
is white sand escaping through the cracks
between my fingers.
I read your work and I am Cinque
swimming against all odds toward the sun.
It overtakes me.
I sink into your oceans of metaphor.
Your poetry, an onion
bringing burning tears to the eyes.
They call you black,
you bring to light the ideas of
black beauty and pride.
They call you savage,
you teach them civilization.
I bury myself in your folds,
layer by layer,
I need to knead your poem,
search for the meaning behind
each word of Wolof,
each image, each simile
sorting, stretching
peeling away surface definition
for the message underneath;
Your voice echoed in our ears
even after you were lowered into the ground.
Your words linger in the air
like dust off of a new drum skin.
They resound like the beating of the dyung-dyung;
a drum sounds for your toiling peasant people,
a drum sounds for Africans all over the world,
Le son du tam tam pour la negritude.

Pig Alley to Mo Mart: Paris Noir

This is Langston's neighborhood
where the rose swam
in champagne till dawn.
       There is jazz here.
I fly over "Pig Alley"
with a wrought iron rail in my grip.
Van Gogh's pre-psychedelic swirls of color
dance with Madame Josephine,
her beauty Black,
her blues bouncing betwixt
the cathedral glistening white,
et la Moulin burning red.
       This is Montmartre,
Little Harlem,
where cobblestones curve
under my feet;
       C'est Paris Noir.
I hear Bullard's horn.
I see Bricktop's red mane.
I feel my people,
unshackled for the first time
on this hill with a view
that stretches farther than the memory
of those Blacks that once lived here.
The tour guide speaks of June Cleaver days.
She has no idea where she's brought me.

Ghost Writer

I chased the ghost of Langston through
crowded streets where drivers moved
like suicide was on their to do list.
I yearned to feel the way I did
when I first read *A Dream Deferred*—
the hair rising on my arms, tingle sliding down my spine
like it does when the dead walk in.

I was looking for Langston
in the trash-filled streets
littered with seeds of urban renewal,
the high rise apartments, the time square billboards.
I looked for him in the faces of New Yorkers.
Each nose, each pair of lips, each set of eyes
spoke volumes about those who couldn't melt
into America's pot.

I chased Langston's ghost in this place
where there was no white, but
Italian, Jewish, Russian,
where black was
Ethiopian, Haitian, Senegalese;
I chased him to Little Africa
where the beat of the tom-toms could be felt
as people spilled out of Africa Kiné
with the scent of lamb mafé in the air.

I finally caught a glimpse of him
in the eyes of a vendor on 125th.
I felt him as I leaned on wrought iron rails
of brownstones in Hamilton Grange,
I saw him in an eighty-something year old man
tap dancing at St. Nicks Pub.
He was with me at the Apollo, the Cotton Club,
We had a finger-licking feast at Sylvia's.

He whispered to me as we walked along the Hudson—
one more river he had known.
We shook our heads as a French woman
scolded her American beau at a black history exhibit.
This is your country, how could you not know?

Finally, I had found the ghost of Langston, so
I sat in Magic Johnson's café,
pressed my pen to paper,
and let the black ink fill the page.

Harlem Moon

I want
the moon
to slip on her
little black dress,
come out with me,
and make the night shine.
I'm tired of using televised
voices to drown out the si-
lence. The moon knows what I
mean. The sun never sticks around
long enough to keep her company. I
want to step out despite the sounds
of sirens, stray cat cries, woman-
bashing bass beats and thug cursing.
Let's go somewhere where I
can close my eyes and
dream of an earlier time
when midnight-skinned men
loved and could wring
pleasure from a woman
until it spilled out of
her like rain.

His Face

~for Mory Thiaw

Eyes—
Golden in the sun,
deep purple when
mixed with moonlight.

Skin—
obsidian, in its cool smoothness,
ebony shaped by
bones like soapstone
chiseled by the most meticulous
of artisans.

Hair—
divinely counted, every one
black, curved by
God's hand.

Diamond smile—
a blinding light
perfect
as an angel's view of
morning.

Note: Inspired by Jean Toomer's "Face"

Color Struck

There is power in this:

I paint hieroglyphics in oil-
turquoise and gold winged Isis
loving her Osiris,
ready to build nations
on the curve of his back.

My hands follow the pleasure in his voice,
knead his skin like dark clay—
we are caramel to chocolate
lavender to purple
morning to midnight.

My hand is the color of sunrise
over a dark ocean.
My fingers, the stars,
cross the moonlit night
between his shoulder blades.

A goddess, his joy in my palm.

Beyond the Brownstones

I sit outside Malcolm's masjid
imagining white veiled black women
and men that don bow ties like suits of armor.

I dream up this lock step brigade,
envisioning the story Spike told of
their fearless march.
Did Malcolm really command them with
the move of one mighty hand?

Black "enuf" bullies can't see me,
my roots unrestricted as
I cheer on the suited army.
Crabs snap, mistake post-black
for post-racial,

but don't even understand
the names of the avenues and boulevards
in this brown-stoned town.

They can't feel the heart of our people
beating on 116th or
understand the holy words
of El Shabbazz

that live in the God-coiled ropes
that crown my head,
and they don't know my soul
sprouts wings and flies

when my feet grace the concrete streets of Harlem.

Get Back!

The city street, lined with brick row homes
is dark but for the dim glow from one window
vibrating like flames to the beat,
the rhythm, the bass pumping from within.
It beacons you, the heartbeat of your people.
You hear them inside, their foot stomps and
            ooowah, ooowah!
You see them on the backs of your eyelids,
afros tight, jive turkeys, hair conked and ready,
thick hipped sisters swaying like Caribbean breezes.
            R-E-S-P-E-C-T, Find out what it means to me!
The Queen of Soul draws you closer,
her powerful voice already
slipping deep curves into your back.
You're there now; You open the white screen door,
lift your strong black fist, blistered and ashy
from holding "I Am A Man" signs all day,
then you notice it—
a brown paper bag tacked to the door;
Thin, fragile, loud, bold,
screaming like the eyes of a southern waitress
when you walk past the "whites only" sign.
In the city where all men were declared equal,
brotherly love fails this simple test.
The chants from the party can be heard clearly now:

> *If you're light, you're all right*
> *if you're brown, stick around*
> *but if you're black . . .*

The Had Generation

Eyes wide, I watch minstrels
and wonder where we went wrong,
these black faces,
full of zip dandy dreams
spit ignorance from their lips like watermelon seeds:
      "The word 'nigga' don't bother me."

Khaleeq plays the Sambo role in class
to black-out his inadequacies;
His hair locked, his mind closed
like the chains on his mentality.
"Lost," Malcolm called it.
Hoodwinked. Had.
His pride, shanghaied.

His name is hood-speak
for "Feets, don't fail me!"
The ancestors ran for freedom,
but he runs without eyes,
a spinning compass, no direction.

I envision his past life;
the lazy field hand,
flirting with Miss Ann,
running and getting caught,
telling Massa' where to find
the Underground Railroad for
a blanket, some extra scraps,
dreaming of being a house slave one day.

For Khaleeq, ambition is for Ol' Massa's clan
as if blackness was measured in food stamps
at the local welfare office.
What will it take to revive his long-lynched pride?
Eyes wide, I watch and wonder
how to encourage him to run, to reach,
to have the audacity of hope?

Broken:
The Toby Effect

Her accent is thick as the beeswax
slicking my naps back,
yet she calls Philly home.

Green peeking out from cracks in the concrete,
she is complete
with the hip switch and eye roll
every ghetto girl needs.

Bone straight Asian hair
hangs from her head,
probably sold by a woman with eyes rounded
by a latexed hand.

This girl is Queen Sheba without her caravan.
A river ancient and wide,
polluted and dying,
born of my mother but afraid to cry for milk;

She's from *Fil—ah—del—fee—ah!*
Struggling to pronounce each letter in the word.
Her eyes beg me to stop asking,
stop calling her "sister."

Black knuckles say that the lightening soap is working.
She puts in ear buds to drum out my voice
and the acidic words hurled at her on playgrounds in the
so-called city of brotherly love.

The Hand that Fed Her

A rabid bitch,
teeth bare and dripping,
venomous words
stunk as she barked into
my voice mail.
Every flesh ripping word
meant to bite me for some
unknown wrong;
Shit thrown to shatter me,
like her fragmented mind,
but the infectious part,
the part that sunk in and itched
the part that boiled up and pussed,
burst through the phone, seeping
and mephitic was

> You call yo-self a 'sistah?'

The last word wrapped in quotes like a lie
foamed up in her mouth,
slid out with her snarl,

> Since you so buh-LACK . . .

She pulled back the word and
snapped it against my brown skin

> You need to fix this, fix this, fix. This. Sh-yit!

The words swung ring 'round rosie
like her essays—no thesis, no main points—

> 'cuz you KNOW you made that class too hard,
> and you KNOW I was on my game!

—the run-ons, the fragments, the misspelled words—
She went on to threaten my parents,
and stalk my cherry-brown boy.

> You call yo-self buh-LACK!?!

She snapped and pictures formed
in the dark spaces behind my eyes,
memories of so-called sistahs
burning brands of "oreo" and
turning words white in my mouth.
Scarred as a slave refusing his name change,
I bit black;
muzzled the bitch,
let the rope she'd laid
snake down around her own neck,
but before I replaced her voice with dial tone
I took a bit of her advice—

> Why don't you stick that in your book? she barked;
> Since you so buh-LACK, write a fucking poem about that!

Ostracized

Do you feel it?
It's in her side glance,
then the whispers that end in
a laugh louder than any joke that was told.
It's the back that turns like a door slam,
the dismissive high pitched "teh" and
the drawn out "mmmmmhmmm"
with the French knob twisted mouth.

Like a key with misplaced grooves,
You're locked out.
For her, the sight of you hurts;
Your smile shines light on her tears,
and hard Rs at the end of words
are like a blow to the gut.
She needs to make you flatten your nose
against the glass;
feel your otherness;
because if they knew that you and she were one,
they'd know she could have done more,
Strived for more, achieved more.

And she fears you know this,
and she fears you know,
and she fears you,
And she fears.

Aunt Rosie's Gift

Eyes closed,
I saw her, as if through water.
She had lost decades, her thick hair black,
her figure shapely, tall, straight,
untouched by age.
She lifted a smooth hand,
smiled, waved and faded away.
Eyes opened,
I heard her; She'd soon be going home,
so I went to her, the keeper of the tales,
our griot, rich with family stories.
Eyes clouded,
mind clear, she spent her last words on me:

> *I used to sit at the feet of slaves*

she told me, the crackling vibrato
fighting cancer's hand on her throat,

> *They were my uncles, my aunts,*
> *my loved ones.*
> *I sat on their laps. I heard their stories,*
> *They turned their backs, and I touched their scars.*
> *This isn't history to me.*

She left me photos, she left me names, she left me words
I left her bedside; she lifted an
arthritic hand and waved goodbye.
My eyes opened.

Big Mamma Blue

Big Mamma
swings that sax;
makes it tell her story.
That sax sings the blues for Big Mamma.

Miss Anne got her trapped in
a box marked "mammy"
where she's
     baby's milk,
     morning breakfast,
     clean floors,
but if Miss Anne could hear
the wave emerging from the mouth
of that horn,
she'd know she was being sassed;

She'd know she was being kicked
by Big Mamma's big black boot
tap tap tapping
to the silken sound of her horn's tearful moan.

Big Mamma kisses her sax
gentle as a lover,
breathes in the Virginia air then
blows all the pain in her full belly
through its mouth;
Her breath, a tornado tamed by
fingers on gold lacquered keys.

Its piercing wail hits hard
enough to straighten
the coils of her hair
and make them dance like the ancestors.

Big Mamma plays, the air turns blue.
Flowers bow their heads in respect,
and the muse offers a rope of
hip moving melody
to carry her out of the box
and on toward freedom.

One of Aunt Rosie's gifts: Big Mamma Blue

Virginia Slims

I stare at sepia-toned "dapper dans"
imagining color
like the green, gold, and brown
that used to dance in the one man's eyes.
He was Charles Henry,
my grandfather's father.
The 80 year old photograph
hides his hazel orbs.
I stare at these cool cats.
Charles leans on his cousin Elvin's chair.
These sons of house slaves don
three piece suits, patterned silk ties,
cigarette holders and spats.
In silence they speak of jazz.
I can almost hear the syncopated foot tapping
on the art deco tiled floor.
They were eye candy for flappers;
Harlem chic in Newark's streets.
I wonder if they were there for the riots,
the day Newark burned over dice,
black and white.
I question them but they sit quietly in my hands.
Their faces tell the story.
Cousin Elvin's slight smile melts into me
while my great grandfather glares,
expression like granite.
Migration from Jim Crow to Jersey ghetto
made him tough as meat on the fire too long.

The Virginia Slims: Charles Henry Hatcher
and his cousin, Emmitt Merrill.

Lost In Time

~for my grandmother

Near the end of her life, Consuela's
frizzy grey hair was thick and black,
spilling over her shoulders
as she peered out at an endless sea
of sunflowers
Her curved arthritic fingers were straight
Her wrinkled skin, soft.
She could hear her father's laughter,
then a voice—
"Mommy? Do you hear me?"
The field shrank and morphed into a
stark white room.

Near the end of her life
Consuela would watch her
three brothers and five sisters
playing outside her window.
They'd call her to come out with them,
then fade away one by one when she refused to go.
The faint sound of a silky voice
singing *Stormy Weather* brought her back to a place
where a pretty colored gal in scrubs
called her "Miss Connie"
and wished her a happy eightieth birthday.

Near the end of her life
Consuela saw a dapper dan
dark as espresso with a brilliant white smile.
He called her "grandma!"
How insulting,
like her triflin' sisters, running around with colored boys,
while calling her "Ol' Black Shang"

for the way her skin turned bronze in the sun.
The hot sun, the cotton pricking her fingers—
Don't let the blood drip in the cotton!

Near the end of her life
Consuela saw a man in a white coat
and knew one day she would wear one.
One day these hands would fix people,
like the full-bellied woman she watched
grow faint in the Texas heat.
Today, the curtain around her bed is a cotton field
and she's been working like a slave
amongst the singing colored folks,
struggling to make quota
with thorn pricked hands.

Near the end of her life Consuela heard the
drip, drip, drip
of the I.V.
beep, beep, beep
of machines
drip drip
the blood dripped in the cotton
the woman squat, pushing, pushing
screaming, pushing,
the bloody baby dropped
in the cotton.
Get up and pick your quota!

At the end of her life
Consuela had become
a little Spanish-speaking girl
in Waxahatchee, Texas.
The walls of her hospital room
were stucco and lined with sunflowers
When the cock crowed she'd

tuck her thick black braids
under a straw hat,
hop into her overalls,
march to the oil fields
and demand a job.
A man's job,
because no matter what happened
she'd never pick cotton again.

Café on Market Street

We sit properly in our designer suits
pinkies out, venti cups tipped
sipping the burnt nectar of bitter beans.
We don't acknowledge where they came from.
They've been splendidly sweetened and pressed
like us, dressed to impress the town's
movers and shakers.
Hob knobbing, rubbing elbows,
we sit and sip in chairs that rest
on the carpets that mask the concrete
that shields our feet from the soil
that was watered with our ancestors' tears.
We sit, sip, chew the fat and forget
that our futures were built on their legacy.
I feel them around me
their eyes, black as these beans,
heritage, rich as this aroma,
hearts, twice as bitter,
for this was the place where their
humanity was stolen
where they were checked for lice, good teeth
and virginity,
where they were torn away from their families—
the wailing mothers' voices still hang in the air.
Still we sit, we sip
the burnt nectar of their bitter beans
and don't acknowledge where they come from.
We don't remember who cultivated
this drink that has become as fundamental as breath.
We don't even know that this street was named for them.

In The Spotlight

Mine was the only brown face in the room
at a charming café where visual art
owned any space that wasn't windowed.

There was a conquistador-colored chica
with a British last name,
an orphan Annie looking woman,
old blue and hazel-eyed men;
and me.

It's the story of my life, so I don't mind it.
In fact, I love the attention, watching elitist faces
go from ivory to pink when they
realize that this isn't just "Def"
but poetry too.

So I spit, as we say. I recited and read;
I unleashed my inner griot;
I was Negritude and Harlem,
Black Arts and Spoken Word.
Womanist—purple to their lavender.
They drank my coffee-colored stanzas and
loved me.

Then ignorance stood boldly and smiled.
She was a back-handed slap with a French accent;
She said I inspired her to read the next poem:

> "I vish I had a big black maman;
> She'd sit on zee porch,
> with her great bosom
> She'd serve lemonade and
> make me think everything will be all right . . ."

Collective gasp; Green-eyed boy laughed.
Chica's cheeks rose red.
Hazel and blue eyes rolled away
carrying the shame for this strange woman
that spit fire from behind the open mic.

I thought about her home,
once the black poets' utopia,
that jazz-land, arts Mecca,
now surrounded by a garden of flames planted
by enraged brown people
like me,
the only one in the room.

Connect

Where is that intellectual space
for obsidian thinkers
where noses open to the scent of java,
black as the depths of the Motherland;
where neo-soul envelopes heavy words;
where heads uplift ideas,
watch them fill the air light as laughter,
breathe them in,
strong and thick as hookah smoke.
Ebony thinkers drum up Harlem thoughts;
My third eye rolls down Lenox Avenue
picturing the days when we were the talk
of the sharecroppers' field.
Today's New Negroes go pomo
reclaiming the right to be ourselves—
the offspring of black fists and black firsts.
We need spaces where boho clad
intellectuals can vibe dread to dread,
palm roll thoughts on education,
Afrocentrism, slams, the 99,
but we're sprinkled through the suburban landscape,
longing to connect with souls that don't
let pop culture mask true culture
and parade around as identity.

Hoodwink Cafe

Hot lattes, soft jazz, Tuscan décor, free Wi-Fi,
and yet nothing can turn this place into a coffee house;
Not even the discount store prints of Parisan café scenes
can make the scent of hot coffee overwhelm the
smell of processed cheese wafting through the air.
No liberals gather here, no original art, poetry,
or intellectual conversation.

This place reeks of ex-cons and high cholesterol.
Every employee, young, ghetto and black,
except for the overly tattooed overseer,
a graduate of Burger U, who looks like she
clawed her way out of an Appalachian trailer,
rolled down mountain through a few bar fights
and into jail where the "coloreds" she met
were far nicer than Pap had told her they'd be.
The golden arches on her clothes make her feel royal.

Her newest field hand is older than the rest and supersized.
She talks loudly as she sweeps the floor of the dining area,
unable to scrape her generalizations
into the dust pan before they are heard.
Bathed in French fry grease and special sauce,
hate spills from her lips like the fat
rolling over her waste band.

Those Muhammad people! They drop eggs everywhere!
She goes on about how they all have
ten wives and want to kill Americans.

Pretending to ignore this mis-educated chick,
I tweet corporate,
squawk about anti-Semitism, then take my own
Muhammad by the hand, my so-called egg,
18 months old, and tell him we'll find another branch
to perch on from now on.

Buggin'

A Christian friend warns me that
the bees drilling holes
in the bricks above my door
might be African.
They don't make sweet honey
they just sting, she says.
I hear them buzzing
like the sounds of Arabic muttering
from my fiancé upstairs—
Up, down, up, down
I hear him change positions,
his words slurring together
as he rushes through.
His rituals scare her
like the bees outside.
Her judging eyes sting.
She fills her week nights
and Sunday mornings with
entranced dancing, fortune telling,
tongue-speaking like a loin-clothed animist.
The praises go up, the blessings come down.
His prayer time ended, he comes down
to see her drilling dogma into my head,
trying to conjure the voodoo
that once made me a drone—
one of the many congregants
blindly serving a self-proclaimed bishop,
the Queen Bee living off of our hard work and tithes.
Up, down, up, down
went my emotions as I dug for
God in that place,
that so-called sanctuary.
I don't heed my friend's warnings.

I tell her I'm happy being
un-churched and spiritual,
She fans away the cloud of bees
that meet her outside my door and
I know my private life will soon be
the buzz of her church's back pew.

Libation

I awoke at the witching hour
as the fringe of a hurricane
battered our sleeping tent.
Only desperation had the power
to force me from my cocoon.
I put on boots and trudged through
mud to the woods.
I could feel their eyes.
I imagined Tolkien's "Ents" peering
down at me in judgment,
or hiding grey ghosts behind their mighty trunks,
their transparent hands ready
to reach out and grab me at any moment.
I mumbled a prayer quick and quiet
wondering if ancestor or angel
would carry my message to Yahweh,
if Allah would listen to a sinner
ankle high in mud, hoodie replacing hijab,
if the ghosts would respect my inner light.
With a gospel humm
I shook off their gaze,
hid behind a tree
lowered myself to the holy ground
and baptized it with my golden stream.

Rant of the Back Slider

Evangelical men use ancient texts,
twisted, sifted and strained through time
to define our womanhood.

These men want us to hide under church steeples
working on their agenda to
capture souls with false promises
about their cure for all of life's problems.

As we run the choir, teach the Bible study,
organize the fundraisers, direct the Easter plays,
they teach us to suppress the questions in our minds—
The why, how, when, who
will fulfill our Cinderella fantasies.

They say it is our fault.
More faith, more good deeds,
more time away from building our own lives
would bring to fruition our Boaz,
our fairy tale, the one God would drop from the sky—

that honest, loving, church-going,
Black man, currently childless,
willing to wait for sex, hardworking,
high achieving, dominant and
respectful at the same time.
If only we'd submit,
had enough faith; paid our tithes.

Lies.
We deserve something real,
not the endorphin-boosting dance
passed down from born-again slaves,
Not self-medicating fat produced
by pancake prayer breakfasts and chicken dinners,
Not ancient words never intended to be taken literally.
Shake the shackles from your third eye.
God speaks. Listen to her.

Addict

~ for C. L. Ross

I heard her story through slurred words
blood shot eyes and ripe breath,
tongue dripping with anger and pain,
and I knew
this was not a moral issue.

One life forever altered
in the time it took for light
to reflect off the tip of a scalpel.
First a cancer and then
a slip, a mix up, a tragic error.
Intestines became tentacled demons
ripping away, sliding out
inflamed, throbbing
like her emotions against
her would be saviors—

the men in white who said
they could fix her,
the blue cross that claimed
it would cover her,
the angels that refused to take her.
Her body cries out so loud
she can't hear anyone else.
This isn't about class or morals.
This is about silence.

Double Whammy

~for Shaashawn "The Voyce" Dial

A black woman was fired without cause
by an organization with a history
of racism and we were silent,
except for the whispers.
"It was her own fault; She shot herself in the foot."
The vast grapevine grows in ghettos
through suburbs,
crosses the Susquehanna and
climbs each rolling hill;
it bursts into churches,
sweeps through corner stores,
but whispers don't act.
This wasn't one of those
NAACP, Al Sharpton
what-would-Jessie-do
type of moments.
"She deserved what she got."
She was unashamedly black,
unapologetically
gay.
Even crowned church mothers
who insist they're still "colored" say
"Ain't no crime, this ho
mo phobia."
Whispers sink deep into the community's fabric
Black words cut through us.
Like kente we unravel.
Not Civil Rights but Civil War,
brother against brother, sister against sister;
There is no **We Shall Overcome** for them,
no Marcus, no Malcolm, no Martin.

Black or not, they are mocked,
and the old warriors fall quiet
as grandmothers' say,
"Hate's ok when the victim is gay.

It just bees dat way."

Woman

Creators on earth,
we are rounded like
the rings in a tree,
balanced radially
God's arms
stretching outward
spiraling out
from our coiled crowns
curved hips, full,
demanding space,
built to bring life.
We are karma walking.
We are bushes burning.
Fearfully and wonderfully made,
we are the picture of God.

*"I praise you because I am fearfully and wonderfully made;
your works are wonderful, I know that full well."*

~Psalm 139:14

Someday:
A Dream Poem

A pretty caramel-colored girl
age of three, one afro puff on her head,
squeezes her knees to her chest and
rolls around on the floor like a little ball as
Ledesi's song, "Someday" plays.
Back she rolls, wiggling toes.
She says "gobble, gobble, gobble, gobble!"
Her turkey sounds amuse her and her
laughter shakes her and rolls her again.
I give thanks for the chance to watch her play.
She is beautiful.

My thoughts are interrupted by a group
of women pushing me to get the birthday cake.
Three cake boxes appear in my hands.
One was damaged on the way, I say.
The cake inside broken in 3 pieces.
They push me to the kitchen where we
squish the pieces back together.
Someone tells me my husband is coming!
The party grows larger. The cake takes shape.

A chili pepper? I ask, though its white, not red.
A tadpole? But again, not green.
We women stare at it in wonder.
It has a head and a tail—
Suddenly I recognize it and
someone yells "Get the eggs!"
The scene fades away
but the little girl's laugh still hangs in the air.

Hormonal Dreaming

Pregnancy unlocks those doors
hidden, bolted, guarded
in the back of my sleeping brain.
In the night I burst through them,
reclaiming old expectations of my life;
I become minister,
corporate exec,
skinny, clothes too big,
the other woman,
thick, curvy, nipples pointed
towards God.
I was even an egg noodle once—
slipping past peas and carrots,
sinking deep into pools of cream soup,
dodging the mercury-laden tuna with agile grace
then fork stabbed and
flown into the mouth of a hungry
baby.

The Crash

The blood is brown now,
soaked into the cracks in my heel.
My bruised belly blocks
efforts to reach it.

Can't scrub it out,
like the memory
of peering down into a
Pollock painting,

pool blue glass
on black canvas,
splattered with red,
framed in the smell of rubber and flame.
This was no abstract.

I spilled onto concrete
trembling, screaming,
holding my middle-
swollen, purple, far too still.

Move, I begged, or take me with you.

Belly

Guttural sounds,
Nose scrunched up,
Face twisted,
Mischievous grin,
Tiny outstretched fingers press
against the wall of flesh
he called home less than
two years ago.

These lines mark the days
I held his growing body.
Once taut, it now it hangs deflated
across my middle.

Did the creams, the dark clothes,
the uncomfortable girdles
speak to him, saying

This is not the warmth that enveloped you
The pillow that cushioned you
The armor that shielded you
This is the shameful, hidden part of me.

Making History

For Andrew Hatcher and the Family

My cousin Andrew was the first
black man in the white house
with a job that didn't require
rubber gloves.
A press agent ignored by the press
A public affairs specialist kept from the public.
He's a one liner in the history books,
a blip on the screen
of Black History Months gone by.
One Ebay auctioned cover of Ebony
lost in the archives,
lost to our family,
to our people.
I wonder if he ever dreamed
that change would finally come?
When he demanded that negroes
be admitted to Princeton,
when he reported JFK's assassination,
when he watched them take Bobby, too,
could he have ever hoped for you?

Nigrescent

A sponge absorbing rainbows,
veiled mirror,
Rising flood of liquid gold,
drivers drowning in its barrels.
A cat in his ninth life, carrying the fate
of those in its path.
Humanity's birthing room,
the Rebirth at 125th and Lenox.
Revolutionary poems spit in brick walled venues,
Reggie Gibson in mud cloth
hands on djembes, dyoung-dyoung, tom-tom,
synthetic syncopated rhythms of
old school hip hop, afro-pop,
Sumatra, no sugar, no cream.
Making greenbacks, debt free.
Listed for avoidance, shunned.
The red chip's nemesis,
the eclipsed sun.
Trailer court girl with daddy issues,
asymmetrical hair cut,
earrings half the size of her head.
Jill's life golden, Lauryn's sun-dipped words
Rasta rhythms, rude boys, jerk chicken
fat back, catfish, cornbread, collie greens
the pentatonic scale, Lucille
and the president of the United States.
(Don't worry. The house will stay white on the outside.)

Waiting For Change

Harrisburg, Pennsylvania March 2008

I don't know what fueled the fire
that kept us from shivering
in the cold shadow
of the cathedral that morning.
Our breath was steam
rising in crisp air,
everyone's eyes were like stars.
We met on State Street, more than 2000 strangers
laughing at ourselves for having this spark,
for being this eager, this excited, this enthralled by
a political process that we'd thought
had forgotten us.
Something in our bellies
made the goose bumps meaningless,
sealed our commitment to
wait for hours on the border of winter and spring.
We stretched our necks to count the city blocks
between our hands and those golden tickets.
Reporters stopped, shocked that we were there.
They had given the keystone to our opponent but
we had come
to build stories for our grandchildren.
Behind me the crowd grew four blocks back.
In front, it stretched four blocks ahead.
The glass was half full now.
I could hear the passersby
as they honked and waved in support.
Someone tossed a "Fired Up!" into the air.
Other voices rocketed into the atmosphere,
"Ready to go!" bounced between office buildings.
"Yes We Can!" zig zagged through alleys
and crept into windows of the undecided.

Forty years after the death of King
hope was alive again
in the tears of Civil Rights veterans
who remembered walking out of John Harris High
on April 4, 1968,
and remembered marching down State Street
to the capital,
and remembered the fires set in frustration.
This chilly morning Hope
was resurrected in unexpected
corners of the Commonwealth—
the blue collar baby boomer,
the newlywed African immigrants
the interracial ghetto family
the gay activist
the black nationalists
the Jewish grandmother
and nose-ringed college kids.
We met in this line, four blocks ahead, four blocks behind
half way to history, huddled together
with strangers
in the hopes of building a
more perfect union.

Armed and Dangerous

My rage-red Saturn
stands out in the traffic jam;
grey street, grey day,
empty train tracks a few feet ahead.
The highway's overpass littered with cars,
stopped, exhaust reaching up to heaven
as if to choke the dead.
The voice on the radio says
the highway is blocked because
of a high speed chase,
four police, three gunmen
on this highway that surrounds
my neighborhood, only a mile away.
Buppie worries invade my brain.

> *I hope the guys aren't black.*
> *If they are, I hope they don't show*
> *their pictures on TV.*

The bar comes down and lights flash
on the train tracks ahead.

BREAKING NEWS—
> *One man is dead, one has been captured,*
> *one is at large, armed and dangerous.*

I see the flat bed trains roll by slowly.
They carry tanks, like in the movies;
Their paint, green as jungles,
brown as desert sand,
their chained wheels, heavy,
long guns, cannons on top;
I think of the young men, boys really,

sent to fire those weapons,
sent to kill other young men,
and those here on the wrong side of these tracks
running from the police.
I wonder if we'll ever get off of
this road we're stuck on.

Paranoia

Sitting in the Wifi-free café
I stare at the document on my laptop
as intruding blues and greys fill my peripheral vision
I prejudge them judging me.
Their pores are clogged with Limbaugh's
rushes to judgment.
They believe in fiery white preachers
who damn old women and little kids to death
for permitting Mardi Gras, miscegenation and voodoo.
Their whiteness blinds the corner of my eyes
and all I see are thin lips whispering warnings
about me and my kind to their children.
I hear the questions they haven't asked
about this 'nappy headed ho'
trying to look smart
with a lap top and no Wifi.

> What school let her in?
> What agency paid her way?
> Did my tax dollars get her that laptop?
> She types fast for a, you know,
> maybe she's a secretary.
> Why does she wear her hair that way?
> Why does she wear Africa on her T-shirt?
> She probably supports that racially-charged
> pastor-
> Why are they so angry?
> It's history!
> Why can't they let it go?

In the corner of my mind's eye
all of their collars are blue, their necks, red.
They watch Seinfeld and feel sorry for Kramer
dream about the good old days when they could say
what they wanted to a nigger who didn't know his place.

The muzak goes from white covers of black songs
to the real "Rick James, bitch!"
And they whisper
as my blackness makes my backbone slip
a groove into the art deco café chair.
They stare.
I hum, loud.
I type to the rhythm they wish they had.
They smile that 'Our darkies are happy here,' grin.
I look up and all eyes roll back to center
to focus on lattes and cappuccinos.
I look down, they roll back to me
and the rhythm with which I thrust
letters onto the screen
       Maybe she's writing a manifesto,
       a racially charged sermon,
       or a plan to take over our picket fenced world!
Exasperated by the comments I hear that are never said,
I throw back my head and let the dreads spill from my
red, black, and green cap.
Then I notice the eyes behind me.
Actors on a TV screen, silent,
as closed captioning tells the story.

Revival 1998

Ten years before conservative media heard the phrase,
my church Harambee, was "unashamedly black."
It stood in a mini-ghetto, the ruins left by white flight.
Deacons swept drunks off the church steps
before services and sometimes after,
on Sunday afternoons, as we
emerged from the heavy wooden doors
soaked in shouts and hallelujahs.

Kwanzaa was a year round event then
and our pastor would get fired up
and shout out the names of city councilmen
"a bunch of handkerchief head negroes," he'd say,
commenting on the mayor's "plantation politics."
His sermons never made CNN.

We were unapologetically Christian then
and when we heard that Jeremiah Wright,
the big city preacher, was coming
every pew was taken, the balcony, filled.
From the choir loft I could see the crowd,
black and white,
getting their stomp on, raising hands,
waving handkerchiefs in agreement.

Reverend Wright's patriotism was never questioned
as he told us black was the absorption of all light
and God was light so our blond assistant pastor
was his brother.
Everyone stood and shouted, *Glory!*
as the music ministry played,
and *God is good all the time and all the time God is good!*

The right reverend spoke in full sentences then,
ten years ago in the shadow of the capital.
He wasn't a sound bite or a video clip
repeating one phrase over and over
for the descendents of the now scattered Klan.

Hillary called him one of America's great black voices,
a leader, a role model, and a holy man.
He was a beacon of light to
impoverished communities
touching individuals, not the world,
not interfering with their empire.

So he was praised from the pulpit and invited to
the White House by Hillary and Bill,
but that was then, before he told a black man
to have the audacity of hope;
long before his words were running for president.

Keystone

I thought you had gone,
stayed back in that
cornfield-framed town with
its shutters on bricks and
hitching posts in store parking lots.

I saw you in the market back then,
glaring at me from Amish eyes,
green as hanging trees,
cursing me black as Satan;

I heard you in an old woman's boast
about the "colored" boy skinned on her street,
where beer cans and racial slurs
were once hurled at me from
monster-wheeled pick-ups.

I saw you in the born-agains,
those offspring of hooded terrorists,
rural minds; small, closed, sheltered.

I'm too young to have known you,
outlawed and outcast before my birth.
Great-grandfather fought you during
night terrors with guns in Georgia trenches.
Mother tested you in Louisiana
with a Civil Rights Act and a dream.

But in this place
of rolling blue mountains
and long-burning coal mines
this place where the Union
fought and thought they'd won,
this Quaker land where Washington slept
where Douglass was lead by the North Star—

this is your playground.

African American History

Mouths sealed, arms folded,
they segregate themselves to the
front of the class, but avoid my eyes,
while Africa's children fill the
back rows with whispers.
No village to raise them,
no fathers to lift them to the sky,
maturity is an elusive shadow, far from their grasp.
I vomit truth and it turns their stomachs.

Eyes widen when I speak of
the day Birmingham birthed "Bomingham."
Denise, Cynthia, Carol, Addie Mae
found huddled together, their bones and white lace
mixed with the debris of the 16th Street Baptist Church.
Their murderers, free, as suspicion was the judge of
young black men, melted skin hanging from their flesh
as their bodies swung from the Klansman's noose.
Even whites, "nigger-lovers," became
headless bodies on railroad tracks,
and some educated traded white hoods for white coats
and whispered "Gnats make lice," to sleeping patients
who would awaken with their wombs bound and gagged.

Niggaz and niggers were the same in those days
but now both sides reject it as too long ago to matter.
Their ignorance is a noose.
Slumping under this burden,
the desire to manumit minds
enslaved by this modern minstrelsy,
my mouth is sewn shut, but my pen bleeds.

Dichotomy

"I feel most colored when I am thrown against a sharp white background."
~Zora Neale Hurston, <u>How it Feels to Be Colored Me</u>

Some mornings I rise and
stretch my naps skyward, outward
like a flower in bloom.
These rain-guzzling, God-counted
strands, clenched like a raised fist,
wrapped in the bold, the primary,
the earthy, animal-printed, braided
with red, black and green and
sprinkled with cowries,
blackness hanging from my locks like
ornaments at Christmas.

At work I plant my feet in Harlem,
water my imagination with words,
invoke ebony ancestors,
call out Langston, Zora, Countee, Claude,
sever student's stereotypes,
critique, create, connect cross-culturally,
until she bursts in like a flood—
Laquandra "Late-n-loud," her
afro eclipsing the sun, is fired up
when a white boy calls her "Macy Gray."
I silence her verbal blows, so
she sends terroristic texts.
A white girl looks at me like
my hands are as locked as my hair.

I pull Laquandra out of class and
whisper a Wanda Sykes warning:
       White people are watching you!

Her eyes roll back through time to
women's clubs, cotillions and Links meetings,
Jack & Jill, AKA and paper bag tests.
Her finger juts through white cotton
fields into white women's kitchens.
Her neck moves
                    back
            and
                    forth
between plantation and sharecroppers' field
Her enraged tongue migrates south to north and
    I   Hate.   Her.
        I love her.
            I *am* her.
        I am *not!*

Eyes emerge from classrooms,
coworkers staring, glaring at us
as if we are the same.
I tell her she can write
better than anyone, think
better than anyone, do
better than anyone,
but will amount to nothing
if she can't let the ghetto go.

Tears break through a damn of mascara
leaving a murky trail between us—
One in the house, one in the field—
both feeling like Zora, *colored*
and thrown against a
sharp white background.

Keeping it Real

My blackness kinks in the rain.
Wraps 'round my naps are a matter of pride.
My black is big, bright as harvest's moon,
warm as Africa, resonating like "white" in ignorant ears-
their self-hate determining language;

My black eats its chicken baked,
can't stand Kool-Aid or
rap made after '92.
My black rocks Chicago, Journey, REM;
Yeah, I said it—
My black is losing its religion.

My black swims in Civil Right's after-birth,
tap dances on the grave of Jim Crow.
My black need not bow to
black on black haters in the hood.

They'd rise if they could,
but they can't
till they pull me
down,
      down
          down
They wanna be down with my black, because
my black makes success seem effortless.
They can't see the struggle in getting the degree
and fighting them with their field slave mentalities;
They ass-ume being a house slave was easy.

My black knows the only difference between
a nigger and a nigga is an accent,
a fallacious argument,
and a white record exec's bottom line.

My black's love is too fierce to kill itself with that word,
covered by ancestral scars that grant cred
deeper than the streets could ever give.
My blackness won't be shackled
by small minds or shadowed by their gaze.

My black is uniquely, essentially, and
unapologetically me.